Thoughts and Prayers from the Front Porch Swing

DEBORAH NORTON

Thoughts and Prayers from the Front Porch Swing
by Deborah Norton

Printed in South Carolina, in the United States of America

All rights reserved solely by the author. The author guarantees all contents are original and do not infringe upon the legal rights of any other person or work. No part of this book may be reproduced in any form without the permission of the author. The views expressed in this book are not necessarily those of the publisher.

Unless otherwise indicated, Bible quotations are taken from *The King James Version*.

Cover Design by Narrow Way Design
Back Cover Author Photograph: Adrian Blackstock Gary

Copyright © 2019 Deborah Norton
All rights reserved.

ISBN: 9781691555796

Dedication

This book is dedicated to all those friends whose prayers and encouragement had me taking pen and notebook to the porch swing for jotting down inspiration.

There are too many to list, but please know I thank each one of you for bending Gods ear, for your patience and for cheering me on!

Chapter One

CREATION

Those Hummingbirds!

Oh my, those hummingbirds! We have a feeder just feet from the front porch swing where I sit and watch their antics.

The porch swing is my place of prayer and meditation. Being in the country it is usually quiet and the meadow across the way is serene. From here I can watch butterflies on the butterfly bush or birds in the clump of oak trees next to the drive. The majestic red tailed hawk that claims this area for his food glides on the air above the grassland and swoops at any movement. It is my happy place. Especially during summer. That is when the Hummers are more than active!

Hummingbirds, like the hawk, are territorial. If you get near their food source they will fight to defend it. I usually have three or four birds and of course every single one thinks the feeder is theirs. If one bird is feeding another will swoop in to knock it away. The only time I have seen the feeder shared is when a new baby comes to eat.

Defending the food does not stop with running the birds off. They will sometimes buzz by me with such force that I will give in to their wishes and give up my seat on the swing. It reminds me that God's creatures are important to Him. His eye is on the Sparrow...and the Hawk...and the Hummingbird...

Matthew 6:26 Behold the fowls of the air: for they sow not, neither do they reap, nor gather into barns; yet your heavenly Father feedeth them. Are ye not much better than they?

Sometimes We Need that Reminder

Good morning, Lord. I have to say, You outdid Yourself on painting this mornings dawn sky. Such a beautiful reminder of Your handiwork. Thank You for allowing my eyes to see it and for putting a smile on my face. Sometimes we need that reminder of Who You are.

Thank You for that sweet yellow butterfly. She was a hint of new beginnings and admonition of the command to GO. I will take this memory throughout the day and share the joy of it with those that do not wear a smile.

Sometimes we need that reminder of Who You are.

Thank You, Lord, for the warmth of the sun, the breeze that blows ever so gently and the silence of earth just before it all awakens anew. There is joy found in the birth of this day.

Sometimes we need that reminder of Who

You are.

Thank You, Father, for the burden You put on my heart for the elderly neighbor down the street. He has no family or friends that visit. But he is glad and cheerful when my children take him a holiday meal I have prepared. I share You with him, Lord.

Sometimes we need that reminder of Who You are.

Colossians 1:16 For by him were all things created, that are in heaven, and that are in earth, visible and invisible, whether [they be] thrones, or dominions, or principalities, or powers: all things were created by Him, and for Him.

Behold, it was Very Good

Looks like a perfect day for chasing birds and butterflies! There's a yellow bellied baby bird (say that three times fast!) sitting on the railing of the back porch. Looks like a Carolina Wren. Old enough to be on its own but calling mama for some breakfast. Its fat, chubby body and fluffy white down on its feathers and chirping its heart out with mouth wide open tells me she is newly released and homesick.

Then there's the black butterfly with awesome blue markings whom I have named, aptly, Houdini. The way he comes and goes, appears and disappears so quickly, he must be called Houdini.

Moreover, there's the cat! Confused little darling. Pretty sure I know where she lives but not sure she does. A neighborhood ragamuffin, she should have a crown on her head as regal as she sits with chin held high. Being a cat she knows nothing about property lines and I can't help but adore *"Her Grayness."*

I am so grateful God has given me a love

for the sweet miracles He allows us to witness. Chasing birds and butterflies will afford me the exercise I need to work in today too!

Genesis 1:31 And God saw everything that he had made, and, behold, it was very good. And the evening and the morning were the sixth day.

I was not Hidden from You

When things don't go as I expect them to and disappointment lays heavy on my mind, God reminds me I am not the one in control. It is not my life to plan. I can't just fall down seven times and get up eight...I have to get up eight and keep going. He has a reason for our frustrations; a lesson to be learned. We must dig deeper to find what that lesson is and for me the lesson is usually to remind myself that it is not about me at all. The days my expectations are not met were planned before I was born and I must remember to give God the Glory for everything in that day...including what disappoints me.

He knew me before conception and wrote todays events down in a book. He knows me well enough to know what I can handle and what I will need His help with. The words He wrote was the plan for my life. My favorite verse says it all..."For I know the plans I have for you," declares the Lord, "Plans to prosper you and not to harm you, plans to give you hope and a future."

Psalm 139:13-16 For you formed my inward parts; you knitted me together in my mother's womb. I praise you, for I am fearfully and wonderfully made. Wonderful are your works; my soul knows it very well. My frame was not hidden from you, when I was being made in secret, intricately woven in the depths of the earth. Your eyes saw my unformed substance; in your book were written, every one of them, the days that were formed for me, when as yet there was none of them.

Metamorphosis

Behold the Butterfly. Its life began as a tiny egg (Stage one) and born as a caterpillar (Stage two) slowly crawls toward metamorphosis. It eats on vegetation. It eats all the time and grows until it becomes "too big for its britches" and enters the Chrysalis (Stage three). The caterpillar stage is the longest stage in the life of these unique creations. Some live just a few weeks, some months, some even years. Their main goal is to continue the species. When the caterpillar has completed its growing inside the Chrysalis it emerges as a beautiful butterfly.

Behold the brand new Christian. Her life begins as a baby as a result of her new birth. She watches and prays and fellowships with other Christians to learn the Word. As she studies and grows, the Holy Spirit surrounds her with Comfort and Grace, like a protective

Chrysalis through the growing pains. God transforms His creatures in His time and in His way.

2 Timothy 2:15 Study to shew thyself approved unto God, a workman that needeth not to be ashamed, rightly dividing the word of truth.

The Bridge

One of my favorite day trips in the area I live is to visit Campbell's Covered Bridge. Having been there many times, I know the best time is early morning in the fall. The red pine structure over Beaverdam Creek is especially beautiful surrounded by pale yellow and fiery red leaves. The frigid clear water flows slowly allowing sight of tiny, darting fish. It is a quiet place, but when the fog is hugging the ground it carries the sound of nearby traffic.

Under the protective cover I can almost hear the pounding horse hooves that must surely have shared the bridge with the earliest of that new invention, the car. My imagination tends to blend with the History of this exceptional place. Farmers at one time traveled many miles to this location to the grist mill that was located just a few feet from the bridge. I enjoy History and this memorable place is chock full of it.

I think history might be important to God too as His words testifies to. Begin at the beginning. Genesis, with the creation of the world. The garden with Adam and Eve. The flood. The call of Moses. The Exodus. Ruth. David. Solomon. Elijah. John the Baptist. The beautiful birth of Jesus. Christ's miracles. Jesus' death and resurrection. Ascension. Paul. John and the writing of Revelation. The Bible is a book of History. It can also be looked at as a bridge. A bridge to reconcile us to Him through Christ. History, a bridge, a book. Some of my favorite things. I hope they are yours as well.

Job 8:8-10 For inquire, please, of bygone ages, and consider what the fathers have searched out. For we are but of yesterday and know nothing, for our days on earth are a shadow. Will they not teach you and tell you and utter words out of their understanding?

Time-Line

***noun* (as in life)**

Picture a line drawn horizontally on paper. Now start at the beginning of the line and write, *I was born.* Go to the right a little and write, *graduated high school.* Continue on and write important happenings in your life on the line. This is what we call a timeline. We have always had a personal timeline but I think it was Facebook that brought the word to our attention and made it popular.

The line you picture is an illustration of your life and from beginning to end it is but a whisper. Daily life, week by week or a month at a time it may seem to go by slow, but looking back years ago it has gone by much too quickly. I look back and wonder, *how did I waste so much time?*

People will ask, "If you could go back would you change anything?" Many things I would not change, but there are some things I would. For instance, I would have spent many more years studying God's Word and serving Him publicly. I would have spent more time marveling at His Creation. Teaching my children more intimate details of Christ would have been a priority.

Regrets? No. What would be the value of that? The thing to do now is to move forward with the knowledge that Jesus and I will be upgrading that timeline daily. It must improve. More of Him, less of me. Will your timeline have *God* written on it as an important milestone in your life? Will His name be there time after time through the years? It should. After all, He is the One Who gave it to you.

Philippians 3:13 Brethren, I count not myself to have apprehended: but this one thing I do, forgetting those things which are behind, and reaching forth unto those things which are before.

Chapter Two

THANKFUL

But for the Grace of God

Father, how can I ever express to You how grateful I am for Your Grace? Your sweet Grace has brought me through a lifetime of Brokenness. A life of Sinfulness. Yet You fill me with Your love.

Many times I hear people say, "But for the grace of God go I."

I hope when people say this they are truly thankful.

I believe God gave me a homeless ministry because at one time I *was homeless.* I know how that feels and what it entails. I know how important a clean, dry pair of socks are. So yes, but for the Grace of God go I.

Once upon a time I was in love with alcohol. I loved everything about it. The smell, the taste the way it made me feel. But eventually He took all of that craving away from me and now I know how to pray for an alcoholic. But for the grace of God go I.

The reason I am an advocate for abused children is because I lived through that. But

God made me see there is another way. The abuse stopped with me. I didn't have to abuse my children or grandchildren. But for the grace of God...

Thank you, Father. Your Grace will take me to the beginning of my eternity. It is More than sufficient.

2 Corinthians 12:9 And he said unto me, My grace is sufficient for thee: for my strength is made perfect in weakness. Most gladly therefore will I rather glory in my infirmities, that the power of Christ may rest upon me.

The Prodigal

I can remember a period in my life when I ran from God and all He stood for.

I was beyond angry. Angry, hurt, confused and to the point of just not caring anymore. My life was in a shambles and I wondered, *Where is God in all of this?* Disarray didn't come close to the mess I was in.

I had experienced life this way since a small girl. But now I was grown. Why couldn't I get my act together? I had given my heart to Jesus as a youngster, but I had done nothing to nourish my soul for years. Rather than going to Him to find answers to life's endless problems I turned inward. You know that, *Oh, woe is me pity party for one*? After suffering for years through anguish, adversity and misery, God placed one in my path to remind me of the solace to be found in Him.

This road is not meant to be traveled alone.

James chapter 5 tells us we are to *confess our faults one to another, and pray one for another.* Had I confided in my Christian friends, rather than hiding behind the facade of a smile, I could have come back to Him much sooner. Of course God was ready to forgive me and was waiting for me with open arms! Thank you, Lord, for brothers and sisters for fellowship.

Isaiah 55:6-7 Seek the LORD while he may be found; call upon him while he is near; let the wicked forsake his way, and the unrighteous man his thoughts; let him return to the LORD, that he may have compassion on him, and to our God, for he will abundantly pardon.

Thank You, Lord

The thought that comes to me from the swing this morning is Gratitude. Even through feeling bad the Lord reminds me of such sweet blessings to be grateful for. Cool, light breezes and the quiet of the country. There's a bird calling from our clump of Oak trees that I don't remember hearing before. Carpenter bees and butterflies to keep me company. Hmmm...time to hang the hummingbird feeder. More Grace for time, more favor for allowing me to enjoy these things.

It is difficult when you physically hurt to ignore that pain and start praising God for what is right in your life. It is so much easier to whine and complain. This is when prayer is so important. Make the biggest part of your prayer thankfulness.

Thank You, Lord, for every gift. I will praise You through this storm!

1 Thessalonians 5:18 In every thing give thanks: for this is the will of God in Christ Jesus concerning you.

Angels in the Room

For years I struggled with not returning to a life of Alcoholism. I wanted to serve God complete, whole and sober. I went to the beach with two of my closest friends. I had not been there in years and was as excited as a teenager. One of the ladies turned in early and the other one agreed with me that a late night swim in the hotel pool would be great. We worked up an appetite and decided to order pizza to be delivered. We didn't want to disturb our sleeping friend so we looked for a place in the lobby to have our midnight snack. The only place we could find was a pub. I hesitated. Alcohol. The smell was enticing and the temptation great. I knew if I had just one I would not stop there. The barkeep's name was Kim. She invited us to sit and have our pizza. Making eye contact with her I felt a kinship and she looked as if she knew my quandary. Once settled she inquired, "How long has it been?"

Surprised by her insight I answered, "Four years and I'll have Dr. Pepper, please."

As we stood to leave, Kim offered a word of encouragement. "Congratulations, you have passed the test!"

The next day I decided to write a brief note of thanks to the barmaid for encouraging me to stay sober. When I asked the manager if he would give the note to Kim he told me, "I'm sorry ma'am, but no one works here by that name or description!"

Hebrews 13:2 Be not forgetful to entertain strangers: for thereby some have entertained angels unawares.

He made a Plan... Just for Me

I have a ring I wear occasionally that has words engraved on it. I call it my Promise ring. Here are the words, so many that it is engraved on the outside and continued on the inside. *"For I know the plans I have for you," declares the Lord, "plans to prosper you and not to harm you, plans to give you hope and a future."*

Jeremiah 29:11 has been a lifeline for me for as long as I can remember. It is the main Scripture on my book, *"Angels, Teddy Bears, and Roses."* From an embattled childhood to a struggling married life to a life lived for Him. Just knowing that God thought enough of me to make a plan was something I have held onto tightly. He thought of me. Me, the one who has failed Him so many times.

Frequently there are times I ask, *Why did this happen or Why does it have to be this way?* Then I remember. God has a plan. This is not my life. It is His. He gave me life and I have given it back to Him to Glorify Him and share the knowledge of Him and hopefully follow His design.

Do you know His plan for you? It is to honor Him and follow Him.

Isaiah 55:8 For my thoughts are not your thoughts, neither are your ways my ways, saith the LORD.

No Limits

A couple of years ago my young Grandson asked me, "Nana, when you get skinny enough to get off of that diet, will you make us a Reese's sundae?" I chuckle when I think of this. Guess he thought being on a diet kept me from making one for him. It was a roadblock. A forbidden thing. There were limits as to what I could do.

How often do we put limits on a limitless God? Many times we ask Him for something or ask Him to do something knowing it would truly be a miracle if He came through. So do we *really* believe He can or will? Or are we simply going through the motions?

God is not magical. He is not a genie to grant our every wish. He is the Creator of the universe. The one and only living God. A God Who loves us and wants all that is best for us. We cannot think of even one thing that He can't supply. There are no limits to what God *can do*. But do you put limits on what you believe He *will do*?

I think He will do more for us than we expect, but we must believe. I feel He is proud of His children when they release their faith in Him. I like to speak my faith out loud. Then leave it up to Him to know if it is good for me. His power has no limits. Neither does His love.

Ephesians 3:20 Now unto him that is able to do exceeding abundantly above all that we ask or think, according to the power that worketh in us.

Love is an Action Word

The woman who eventually became my foster mother and the most important person in my life for so many years looked for ways to spend time with me. Because of where my birthday fell in November, I would be almost seven years old before I could begin school. So Mama Mary convinced my mama to let me go to an expensive private school for first grade because they would accept me at age five. She said she would pay the tuition, drive across town to pick me up every day to take me to school and make the same drive in the afternoon to pick me up and take me home. Every day when school was dismissed she was there with a pack of Cheese Peanut Butter crackers and a half pint carton of Pet chocolate milk. Still my favorite snack! She showed her love for me so many times in so many ways.

When I remember this chapter of my life I

am reminded of the *Parable of The Lost Sheep*. Not because I was lost but because of how much I was loved. A shepherd had a hundred sheep and one of them strayed from the fold. The shepherd left his ninety-nine sheep to search for the lost one until he found it. This means that sheep was important enough to him to go out of his way for that sheep. Mama Mary went out of her way for me. Paul tells us, *love beareth all things, believeth all things, hopeth all things, endureth all things.*

Jesus went even more out of His way for me and for you. Because He loves us. Love. Just a word until action is put with it.

1 John 4:10 Herein is love, not that we loved God, but that he loved us, and sent his Son to be the propitiation for our sins.

Chapter Three

WITNESSING

I will Look for Ways to Share You

Abba Father, in praising You today, I will look for ways to share You with others. It may only be a smile or holding the door for someone or saying a prayer, but remind me of the boldness You have blessed me with. Remind me of Your command to GO. You have provided a Mission Field for each of us. We just have to be aware of where You send us.

Someone asked me not long ago, "Where do you think your Mission Field is?"

My answer was swift and sure, "Wherever I am."

I have loved sharing You with the homeless. I have enjoyed my times at the children's orphanage while sharing You and the blessings You have provided for them. Because of the bold desire I now have to share You, I have prayed with strangers on the street. Giving a book of my testimony means more to me than selling one. Singing Your praises at my home church or while visiting another is a two-fold blessing as it is sharing and worship. May we always be aware of those in need of Your touch. Thank You for the opportunities You allow for us to share You through small kindnesses.

I pray You will continue to open doors for witnessing as I believe it is our purpose.

May others look past the clothes I wear. Past the new way I cut my hair or the shoes on my feet. Make *me* invisible to the world Lord so that all they see is *You*!

Mark 16:15 And he said unto them, Go ye into all the world, and preach the gospel to every creature.

It was a Good Day

This evening, Lord, I just want to say thank You. For traveling mercies and protection. For the smile on that child's face. For allowing me to see past the sadness of poverty and see the Hope in that man's eyes. Thank You for the little things and the big things. It was a good day.

He sat in that McDonald's restaurant nursing a steaming hot cup of coffee. His backpack looked familiar and I wondered if it was one that my Christmas Homeless Ministry had just delivered to the shelter downtown. He looked old, probably beyond his years. *He needs a shave,* I thought. *Did all of our back packs get razors?* I wondered. He was skinny, almost frail, and he looked hungry.

We were in a public place so as I sat at the table next to him I asked, "You live around here?"

He looked shocked that I had spoken to him. "No Ma'am," he said. He was quiet, almost timid as he continued. "I used to. Now I live wherever I hang my hat."

"I used to live on the corner across the street," I replied. That started a conversation about how the neighborhood used to be which led to his admitting he was down on his luck and coming out of rehab. "Do you know Jesus?" I asked. He looked down as he shook his head yes and sipped his coffee.

I didn't want to embarrass him so I reached into my purse and pulled out the two five dollar gift cards left over from stuffing those back packs. I nonchalantly asked, "You hungry?"

"Always," he replied.

I slid the cards over to him and still not wanting to shame him I left before he could get back from ordering his food. I prayed for him on the way home. I prayed for him today. It was a good day.

Proverbs 19:17 He that hath pity upon the poor lendeth unto the LORD; and that which he hath given will he pay him again.

Do unto Others...

Good Morning, Father. When I consider the folks you have placed in my path. The young, the old, the sweet, the sour, the strong, the weak. I just want to thank You for every one of them. They have each brought something into my life and it has helped to make me who I am and I appreciate every gift!

It amazes me to think of how many people there are, yet You have made each one different. You place some in our lives that are so easy to love. It just comes naturally to want to spend time with them and want the best for them. Our paths are also blessed with those we find it hard to draw close to, yet there is a purpose for their being there. Some will teach us. Some will learn from us. Some will bless us. Some will test our patience. But because of Your example of pure, Agape love, we can show our affection and devotion to all.

Sometimes a stranger will enter our busy day and without thinking we give the appearance that we don't have time for them.

Help us to remember, Lord, You love this person. Remind us that we want *them* to see *You* in us. This newcomer could very well become our best friend in the world. This is the time to remember, "Do unto others as you would have them do unto you."

Matthew 10:30 But the very hairs of your head are all numbered.

Begin with My Heart

Today's Thought from the swing: Never be so busy that Jesus is at the bottom of your priority list. I sometimes feel that I don't do enough to build on our relationship or express my love for Him.

Sometimes we become so self centered all we can think about is what is going on in our lives at that moment. *Was it a good day at work? Did I remember to put that card in the mail? I really should check to see if the oil change is due in the car. I need to go see Mom.*

All of these things are important and a part of our everyday lives. But nothing is more pivotal than communing with Christ. He talks to us through His word. We talk to Him through prayer. This interchange makes our day go smoother and we can know that whatever happens, He is with us and it brings us peace.

Prayer: In Your time and in Your way, Lord, please begin with my heart. Remove all wrong and heal it completely. Then touch my mind, Lord. Make my way of thinking after

Your way. Mend my body so that I may again freely work for You. Repair my spirit so that I may boldly share You. You are my Healer, Jehovah Rapha, and I long to be healed and Holy and to put You at the highest degree of importance.

Matthew 6:33 But seek ye first the kingdom of God, and his righteousness; and all these things shall be added unto you.

Stay Humble

Life itself is a lesson in Humility. Humility is something we must strive for daily. Sometimes it comes easy...like doing kind acts such as holding the door for someone. Or lending a hand. Or asking, "What would Jesus do?" I like to look at it as, "I am a servant for Christ. How can Jesus and I help you today?"

But sometimes I get full of myself (Yes, I am human) and forget that a humble attitude will shine God's Glory best. It is humbling to me and for me that God will slow me down to remind me of that.

When I have a speaking engagement I sing, then speak and usually talk with people afterwards about the books I have written. Many times the compliments start almost immediately. I appreciate every one of them, but I want God to get the Glory for all that is done in His name. The devil wants me to let those compliments go to my head and leave God out of it. But now when someone acknowledges a song or enjoys my testimony, I say praise the Lord or to God be the Glory! I am striving to show Him and His goodness in every opportunity.

Lord, may humbleness begin in my heart and grow outward. Clothe me with humility for Your sake.

Philippians 2:3 Let nothing be done through strife or vainglory; but in lowliness of mind let each esteem other better than themselves.

Seeing Things Differently

Since my three-year-old grandson already knew how to recite the alphabet, I decided to start teaching him letter recognition. Settling down with his child-sized computer keyboard I asked him, "Sweetheart, do you know what the alphabet looks like?"

"Yes, Ma'am," he replied. "Soup!"

Even as adults we sometimes "see" things differently and not always in a good way. We look at a situation and at people and automatically "judge." Yes, I am guilty. Maya Angelou offered some good advice for just this kind of quandary. *"Do the best you can until you know better. Then when you know better, do better."*

When we find our thoughts going in a judgmental direction, let us ask the Lord to remind us of His command to love others, to help us see things as they are and to withhold judgement. Then let's share the love of Christ in whatever that situation might be.

Luke 6:37 Judge not, and ye shall not be judged: condemn not, and ye shall not be condemned: forgive, and ye shall be forgiven.

What are You Called to Do?

I have heard it said many times. From Mother. From Daddy. From teachers. From friends. "You can do anything you set your mind to do."

I dabbled at writing for years. As a teenager I was all about writing poetry for boys. (Insert shy smile here.)

As a young mother I wrote about the accomplishments of my brilliant children. (Insert proud smile here.)

As I grew older I felt a desire to write for the Lord. I didn't know how to go about it. So He set a friend in my path to show me how and to say, "You can do anything you set your mind to do." She is still saying it and supporting me in her own sweet way.

Confirmation for my writing and speaking came from a local news anchor who is also a published author. You see God will use others to establish and verify what He wants from you. Do what I set my mind to do? I pray it is what He has set my mind to do.

Keep your heart and mind open to the works you do to glorify Him. Keep your ears open to hear His instruction. My work is to point to Christ and Christ alone. Only He is worthy. Only He can provide what is needed.

I pray that as I do the work I am called to do that others see Him in me. What are you called to do? You can do anything you set your mind to do...but only through Christ.

Philippians 4:13 I can do all things through Christ which strengtheneth me.

Go!

I remember an old saying, *Someone needs to light a fire under you!* I heard it a few times as a youngster on those days when I just didn't want to go to school. It meant I was being lazy and it was going to take lighting me up to get me moving. Many times it was true. I did need something drastic to stir up the energy that was hiding deep within. Kind of like when we are called to do something for the Kingdom of God.

Ever been awake at 3:00 in the morning and realize God wants some of your time and attention? I have. I was reminded that He wants us to *Go,* to share His Gospel with everyone. As butterflies fly quickly in every direction, that is how He wants us to go and to share. We shouldn't need a fire lit under us to do this. All that we need to motivate us is inside of us if we have the Holy Spirit in our hearts. Fear cannot get in the way. Doubt cannot slow us down. There is fire within to get started. That fire will burn forever as long as Christ is the Lord of your life. That fire is your motivation. That fire is your light. Go and let it shine!

Mark 16:15 And he said unto them, Go ye into all the world, and preach the gospel to every creature.

Chapter Four

HEALING

By His Stripes We are Healed

Jesus, thank You for providing Doctors, Surgeons, Medicine and prayer for when we become ill. You healed many during Your time on earth. You healed through the power of the most High God. Then You gave that same power to your disciples. I believe, Lord, that power still exists today. I also believe Your Promises come when we are obedient. Help me to be obedient to You always and thank You for the Healing we have asked You for.

When I read in Isaiah, *By His stripes we are healed,* I accept that healing in several ways. First, we are healed for our sin sickness. Because the laws of the Old Testament were strict, it was next to impossible to keep them all. Because we are human and worldly and in the flesh. But God provided for our soul healing with the ultimate sacrifice of His Son and because of that we are allowed peace every day.

Secondly, because Jesus went about healing

folks when He walked the earth and told the disciples they have that same authority. It was because of the stripes He received for us that when we claim Jesus, we can claim all healing!

Isaiah 53:5 But He was wounded for our transgressions, He was bruised for our iniquities; The chastisement for our peace was upon Him, And by His stripes we are healed.

There will be Smiles to Come

Lord, I am missing some people today. Some are with You. Some still walk this earth. Sometimes they cross my mind and that pang of emotion hits hard. It is what happens when you love deeply. I run to You now because You are the Healer of hearts. The only One that knows my thoughts. I give it all to You and thank You for the healing and the smiles to come.

Many will go through this day grieving. Some will bear the physical pain of losing a loved one. Loss of appetite. Unexplained aches and pains. Others will experience depression, denial, anger. Most will struggle with all of this and not just once, but again and again. It is the natural way of things. Death is a part of life. But knowing that doesn't change the way we feel.

Even Jesus experienced grief. John 11:35 said it ever so simply when Lazarus died. "Jesus wept." But I believe He grieved and wept for the loved ones of Lazarus. He mourned because they hurt so.

One thing I am looking forward to in Heaven is found in Revelation. "And God shall wipe away all tears from their eyes; and there shall be no more death, neither sorrow, nor crying, neither shall there be any more pain: for the former things are passed away." Thank you, Father.

Psalms 147:3 He healeth the broken in heart, and bindeth up their wounds.

Finding the Funny

Sometimes life is funny. Who would've *thunk* up such an atrocious combination? An old woman's med's that consists of a blood pressure pill that also happens to be a diuretic and a cholesterol pill that makes you sleepy. I sit up on the side of the bed and immediately go "Whoa!" did I sit up too fast? I don't have time to answer because I have got to "go"!

So I start for the bathroom and BAM! (Who put that door there?) This begins the Pin Ball Machine game and I am the ball. I begin to mimic Barney Rubble from the Flintstones. "*Tink, tink, tink*!" Tiny steps to the left..."*Tink, tink, tink*!" bouncing off the wall to the right. Finally get through the door that somehow has bumpers that keep me literally bouncing off the walls toward the tub. "*Tink, tink, tink*"! Stop! My diabetic feet with the numb spots and freezing toes have found their balance. Right in front of the toilet! Well that was a quick trip! Now to find my way back!

Proverbs 17:22 A merry heart doeth good like a medicine: but a broken spirit drieth the bones.

Be Thou Whole

I was sick recently and had to find a doctor. Rarely do I "come down" with anything but this knocked me off my feet. Well, I was in the doctor's office today for 3 hours and none of it was idle time! I have been poked, prodded, invaded and stuck. She is referring me to a specialist, an educator, a gym and the business office. Maybe I should have stayed at home!

When Jesus walked the earth large crowds came to Him bringing the blind, the lame, the mute. They sought Him for the healing of their loved ones. They fought the crowds and in one instance lowered their loved one from the roof to reach Him.

The Lord laid His hands on them and spoke His healing words over them and to them. But what Jesus really wanted them to know is the healing they needed more than physical healing was the restoration of a sin sick soul. Yes, His powerful touch made their bodies whole, but through their faith and belief in Him and turning away from their sins is what saved their souls.

I believe He is the same yesterday, today and tomorrow and I continue to seek Him for healing. But I am happy to report my sin sick soul is healed!

Matthew 9:12 But when Jesus heard that, he said unto them, "They that be whole need not a physician, but they that are sick."

Oh, but I do Love Food!

Ok, I am going to say an ugly four letter word right here. Get ready. Here goes. *Diet.* There. I said it. Why in the world does that word even exist in the English language? Was somebody really mad at their hubby when they thought up that punishment? I can hear it now. "I know what I'll do. I'll tell him there is this new thing called a *diet* and he has to stay on it till he loses twenty pounds. Then I'll serve him rabbit food for weeks. Teach him to complain about my cooking!"

But, seriously, I do love food. I enjoy cooking and experimenting in the kitchen and am always on the look out for new recipes. It can be tempting to overeat and of course we all do at times. So what does the Bible have to say about this?

1 Corinthians tells us, "What? know ye not that your body is the temple of the Holy Ghost which is in you, which ye have of God, and ye are not your own?" These bodies are on loan to us. They belong to God.

Part of the sanctification process (Yes, it is a process!) is working with the Holy Spirit to display the nine fruits of the Spirit. One of those nine fruits is *self-control.* This is to be applied in every aspect of our lives...yes, even eating. It helps us to treat our temple with respect. Take care of Gods property!

Genesis 1:29 And God said, Behold, I have given you every herb bearing seed, which is upon the face of all the earth, and every tree, in the which is the fruit of a tree yielding seed; to you it shall be for meat.

Hope of Resurrection

Oh, the pain of the loss of a loved one. We can suffer heart break at the loss of a friendship. We hurt when the word divorce is on our lips. We are all sensitive to physical aches and pains. But there is no hurt like the one in knowing a loved one has died. Maybe it is because it seems so final. Maybe it is because we will miss them so much. Could be because we don't understand or know what they have experienced. Whatever the reasons know that God sees our tears and knows our pain

We all go through grief in different ways. Most of us hurt. Most of us question why. Most of us get angry. But individually it may not hit us all the same. Some grieve a short time. Some grieve for years. I might cry hours at a time while you never cry at all. But know that God sees our hearts and the Holy Spirit Himself will comfort us with the Hope of resurrection. Ask for comfort. He is happy to oblige.

Revelation 21:4 And God shall wipe away all tears from their eyes; and there shall be no more death, neither sorrow, nor crying, neither shall there be any more pain: for the former things are passed away.

Seasons

Raise your hand if you have ever climbed out of bed with aches and pains and sore all over! On a regular basis. Yeah, me too. If you are in the "seasoned" age, you know exactly what I am talking about. That *snap, crackle, pop* you hear before you even get to the kitchen! Then that low, awful noise you hear before you realize it is you, moaning and groaning. That's just the everyday physical hurts, not to mention the pang of modern day bills that hit our wallet monthly and the stress of family dilemmas (my Grandson did *what?)* Then, you turn the TV on! Life happens! But there is hope.

The Bible doesn't tell us how long Job suffered through his "season" of suffering. We must assume it was a long time because one of the first things we think of concerning his story is patience. The Bible uses words like *affliction* and *perseverance*. I can't compare my "afflictions" to Job's, but I can look to him as an example of how to handle whatever calamities come my way. *Simply trust God!*

Romans 8:18 For I reckon that the sufferings of this present time are not worthy to be compared with the glory which shall be revealed in us.

Chapter Five

MEMORIES

Tuckers Soda Shop

Father's Day always takes me back to a favorite place and time spent with the man who chose to love me. Daddy's favorite place to eat was *Tucker's Soda Shop*. There were mini juke boxes on the marbled tabletops and I begged to hear the clinking of coins dropped into the tiny music boxes. Chubby Checker belted out *The Twist* while the whirl of the ceiling fans kept the rhythm.

Looking forward to that gooey grilled cheese sandwich only made it better and the fat french fries, too hot to eat, cooled as I coaxed the thick ketchup from the glass bottle. Daddy thought Tuckers hot dogs were the best but I didn't care for the pungent onions on top.

After our meal there was always a treat for me. I would sometimes linger over every comic book in the rack until finally, I chose *the* one. Soon I was poking my nose into its pages, loving the fragrance of its ink.

Sometimes our goody was a scoop of hand dipped chocolate ice cream served in a cone. I usually wore some of it home.

The Soda Shop is closed forever now and Daddy has gone to meet Jesus, but I often visit Tuckers with him in those sweet memories that remind me of his love and patience.

Revelation 14:13 And I heard a voice from heaven saying unto me, Write, Blessed are the dead which die in the Lord from henceforth: Yea, saith the Spirit, that they may rest from their labours; and their works do follow them.

Promises

My memories this morning take me back several years to when my grandson was about three years old. I was telling him about how Jesus is coming back some day to take us home to live with Him. His response? "Wow, Nana. Jesus must have a mighty big airplane!" Out of the mouths of babes!

No, Jesus won't be flying a Boeing 747 when He returns. But His children will be so happy to see Him that it won't matter. As a matter of fact, He ascended in the clouds and will return in the same manner.

There are so many things to look forward to when you serve the living God. He made promises we can count on today, but He also promised us a new home in the after life where there are mansions and streets of pure gold. It's a gated community where we won't need to close the gates. The twelve gates are made of pearl and connecting them all are walls of Jasper. The river of life is pure as crystal and there shall be no more death, neither sorrow, nor crying, neither shall there be any more pain: for the former things are passed away.

In Corinthians we are told, "Eye hath not seen, nor ear heard, neither have entered into the heart of man, the things which God hath prepared for them that love him." I am clinging to that promise!

Matthew 25:13 Watch therefore, for ye know neither the day nor the hour wherein the Son of man cometh.

There is a Friend...

I recently spent the day celebrating a fifty year-old friendship. I blinked and just like that we were not fifteen anymore. My life has taken so many twists and turns it is amazing I can even say I have an acquaintance that old. We were best friends in high school and after a few years of going our separate ways and meeting life head on, we took up where we left off like that break never happened.

Friendships, whether fifty years or one year in the making are so important. Friends help to mold us...to make us who we are. We learn from them; we teach them; we need them. We need them to keep us strong in some areas of our lives and to keep us laughing in others. A friend is the only one that can make me laugh at myself and it's okay. I don't have to have a passel of close friends. If they are good ones, two or three will fill the bill. But there is one friend I need more than any other. Jesus. He is everything I will ever need.

Proverbs 18:24 A man that hath friends must shew himself friendly: and there is a friend that sticketh closer than a brother.

I am Worth Many Sparrows

As an eleven-year-old runaway I remember after a little while of living in the city park I became hungry. I picked up soda bottles on the side of the road and turned them in to the local grocer in exchange for a few pennies each. I could get crackers or candy and a Pepsi. But one day the supply had dwindled to nothing and I was still hungry.

So I dug through my small box of belongings and took the Bible I had with me to a house across the street from the park. After knocking loudly an elderly lady shuffled to the door. Her seasoned smile was genuine but her bend at the waist appeared to be painful. I gathered from first sight of her that she was a lady. Dignified. Her grayed hair coiffured. Her, "May I help you?" encouraged my response.

"Yes, Ma'am!" I said loudly. I figured someone this old was probably hard of hearing.

"I have a Bible here I want to sell."

She looked at me thoughtfully, then said, "Well I just might want to read it."

Just like God to feed an old woman's soul and a little girl's tummy with the same Bible! He is always providing for His children!

Philippians 4:19 But my God shall supply all your need according to his riches in glory by Christ Jesus.

Fat Boy

His name was Fat Boy. Part Lab, part Chow. Black from the tip of his tail to his always wet nose. My family rescued him and his brother. He was a skinny little runt but his thick curly hair made him look like a fat rat!

We almost named him Houdini as he was adept at escaping the kennel with six-foot chain link walls. He climbed like a monkey!

I could never figure out if he just loved being outdoors or was simply afraid of the unknown as I could not get him to come inside. After he was full grown I wasn't fond of the thought of him inside either. You know, *bull in a china shop* kind of thing. But at the ripe old age of fourteen and with ice on the ground I knew I had to get him in.

He had the whole screened-in back porch as his own. There was a fine doghouse with wood chips there and he had all that hair...but still. He was old. He had arthritis. So I pushed and pulled against his groaning and his paws putting on the brakes. I begged. I pleaded. It took awhile, but I got him into the warmth of the laundry room and finally he settled down.

I wonder if this is how God feels sometimes when He is trying to direct our steps. He wants us to be in the best place He has prepared for us but we put on the brakes because we are afraid of the unknown. Next time you feel Him pushing or pulling you to an unsure place...trust Him. He loves you.

Proverbs 3:5 Trust in the LORD with all thine heart; and lean not unto thine own understanding.

Laying up Treasures

One of my children is extremely talented with woodworking. A few years ago he made a chest for me that I call my treasure box. The chest itself is a gem. Its Sangria red stripes and knots against the blond softer wood and its pure cedar fragrance speaks of a time when cedar trees were plenteous. A beautifully carved eagle placed on the front of it adds to the character of the trunk. The things I keep in this prize are mostly memories. Worth nothing in dollar value, but priceless as sentiment goes. There are pictures my children and grandchildren have drawn. Thank you cards, birthday cards and Mother's Day gems. Things that belonged to Mother and small gifts from friends. Endearing, but not my most important treasures.

Now the Bible tells us to not lay up treasures here on earth. But I believe this has to do with material things that we put a lot of value on.

There's nothing inherently wrong with owning *stuff* as long as we don't let it take away from God's tithes or as long as we keep it in perspective. Riches will not follow us to heaven.

Jesus is the number one treasure in our lives. Acts of service to God is a treasure. Keeping His Word and commandments are treasures. What does your heart desire?

Matthew 6:19-21 Lay not up for yourselves treasures upon earth, where moth and rust doth corrupt, and where thieves break through and steal: But lay up for yourselves treasures in heaven, where neither moth nor rust doth corrupt, and where thieves do not break through nor steal: For where your treasure is, there will your heart be also.

Frozen in Fear

One of my earliest memories took place around the age of four or five. I was at my Granny's home, an old clapboard house that had never seen paint, but it was new to me. The sun had gone down and the crickets and tree frogs vied for first place in the *loudest* contest. Then another contender stepped in.

My nine year-old brother decided we would watch King Kong on Granny's black and white television set. He turned the sound up and the screaming coming from that box was topped only by my brothers screeches of delight.

Me? I was horrified. Probably the response the movie makers wanted. I was sitting on the couch and backed against it as far as I could. Then I stood on the couch and climbed onto its back. Standing on the back of the couch, I pushed into the wall as hard as I could trying to get far away from the terror I was witnessing.

Then I froze. I could not move another inch. My internal switch for fight or flight had not kicked in. My realization of what was real and what was not had not matured. I was simply scared. Frozen where I stood.

As an adult I have experienced fear a few times. But since I have come to the knowledge of the power of Christ fear does not last. The Bible tells us many times, *Do Not Fear* and *Fear Not*. We are protected by the creator of the universe. In Psalms David said he sought the Lord and the Lord heard him and delivered him from all his fears. He does the same for us.

Isaiah 41:10 Fear thou not; for I am with thee: be not dismayed; for I am thy God: I will strengthen thee; yea, I will help thee; yea, I will uphold thee with the right hand of my righteousness.

Chapter Six

JOY

Squeals of Delight

The rumble of thunder and white flashes of lightning from a seasonal storm kept me company most of the night. Powerful sheets of rain swept against the house and the wind wailed.

Looking at the aftermath of last nights rain I had a flashback to years ago. My elementary school aged children and I went grocery shopping after a rainstorm. As soon as they got out of the car it was as though the rain puddles were magnets to their little feet! They immediately ran to those mini ponds and oh, the squeals of delight and laughter as they jumped and splashed! My first instinct was to yell, "Get out of that water! You will be filthy!" But I stopped myself before "raining" on their joy. Instead, I went over and sloshed and splattered them all! Then led them inside.

I wonder how many times our Heavenly Father admonishes us to "Get away from that. You will be filthy!"

To *repent* means to turn away from sin and

the evil ways of the world. Twice, Jesus said in the Bible, "Go, and sin no more." In other words, you have been forgiven, do not return to a sinful lifestyle.

If you are feeling guilty about something you are doing, it is the voice of the Holy Spirit you hear. Jesus said the Spirit would be a counselor, leading us. Guiding us into all truth.

He doesn't convict us to hurt us or to "rain" on our joy, but rather to enlighten us as to how we should behave or to show us the path we should *not* follow. He wants to keep us within His parental sight. To keep us safe even as He guides us to a place of delight and laughter.

Romans 8:14 For all who are being led by the Spirit of God, these are sons of God.

Drenched in His Love

Being a writer I often find myself drawn to a word I have heard a thousand times but didn't pay attention to. This morning that word is DRENCH, as in immersion or soaking. Wanting to draw closer to the One that has saved me. Wanting to know His Presence. Bending His ear with how I need His companionship daily the thought came to me that I want to be "drenched in His Love."

I remember a time I thought someone was no longer going to be a part of my life. They were moving on and I was going to miss them terribly. The tears flowed and I decided I never wanted to love someone that much again. Parting was too painful.

Soon, a thought came to me and I am sure it came from Him. *You can't have it both ways!* You see, I had asked God to teach me to love the way Jesus loves. Now I was swearing off loving to avoid the pain of losing someone in my life. I decided loving the way He loves is best. After all, it is not the love that hurts.

Drenched in His love? Yes, I am!

1 John 4:7 Beloved, let us love one another: for love is of God; and every one that loveth is born of God, and knoweth God.

Love Anyway!

Concerning Love. True love means unconditional, free, compassionate, constantly forgiving devotion. I once asked Jesus to teach me how to love. I wanted to love like Him. Be careful what you ask for. Love like His comes with great responsibility. Love like His is a pure gift of caring. Caring about the lives of others. Caring about the souls of others. It comes with great Joy for their happiness. But it also comes with great pain when they hurt. It comes with the price of losing others when they don't love you the way you love them. Oh, but the price is so worth it.

Love is a verb. It is an action word. If you show someone you love them through your actions and they simply don't respond or they ignore your attempt to love them, love them anyway! When God looks at you He sees your heart. He knows that you love.

John 15:12 This is my commandment, That ye love one another, as I have loved you.

Old? Me?

I have children, grandchildren, even great-grandchildren. Lord, how did I get to this place? Where did the time go? I can remember times and days that seem a hundred years ago. Then some seem like yesterday. Sitting on this swing I feel like I am twenty-one again in my mind, but I know I look every day of my old age. I know I should act my years but sometimes it is hard to do because it is much more fun to be young again. I wonder, am I the only one to feel this way? I think not.

Gods word tells us, "Though our outward man perish, yet the inward man is renewed day by day." Benjamin Franklin pointed out, "Those who love deeply never grow old; they may die of old age, but they die young."

Thank you, Lord, for this dividend in the perks of growing older. We can get old, but we don't have to *be* old. It makes a seasoned life so much more enjoyable!

Job 5:26 Thou shalt come to thy grave in a full age, like as a shock of corn cometh in, in his season.

I Know You!

I know him, I thought. *Oh, what is his name?*

I sat in the private dining area of the restaurant with my books, bookmarks and the angel figurine a friend had gifted me with. I had overcome the nerves that used to accompany me at every book signing and was actually enjoying this one.

This man with his steel blue eyes and sun-bleached hair was so familiar. He stood in front of me expectantly. I reached for one of my books and the ink pen to sign inside the cover. My mind was reaching far back into memories long forgot. "Do I know you?" I asked. He smiled a toothy grin. As soon as he opened his mouth to speak I knew. I jumped up from the table and went around to hug the friend I recognized from high school days, many years ago. "Jimmy!" I squealed. It had been a long time, but I knew him.

This is how my hope in Jesus will prove itself someday. He will see me, receive me, recognize me and hug me close as my Savior and Friend. He knows my name and I am looking forward to that day!

Isaiah 43:1 But now thus saith the LORD that created thee, O Jacob, and he that formed thee, O Israel, Fear not: for I have redeemed thee, I have called thee by thy name; thou art mine.

When God Gave Me You

Never question the role of a foster parent or an adoptive family. They play such an important role in children's lives. Not all are a good match, but most children grow to appreciate the love they receive in these families. I don't like to think about where I might be today if my foster family had not loved me the way they did. I could not have loved them more if we had the same blood running through our veins.

I wrote this poem as a tribute to my Foster Mother.

When God Gave Me You
God in His Heavens looked down on that day
At a dirt smudged little girl sitting at play
Knowing my future knowing my plight
Sent Angels to watch me and keep me in sight
He sent down a plan to give me some Hope

A plan not to harm me but help me to cope
A life that would prosper and not live in shame
One that pushed forward and soon overcame
He gave me so much so I would not fall
But when He gave me you He gave me all.

Proverbs 22:6 Train up a child in the way he should go: and when he is old, he will not depart from it.

Soup Anyone?

Cooler weather is just around the corner. Time for a big crock of my homemade vegetable beef soup. Soup. When I think of it I automatically think comfort food. I love it and almost crave it when I am sick. You can usually find bowls of different kinds of soup in my freezer during the winter months. When I am under the weather it is ready for me. Or when a friend is sick it is ready for them. Or when there is snow on the ground that big steamy bowl of thick broth is like medicine for the body.

Speaking of comfort food. There is a cure for a soul that needs rest. It is not found in the freezer but is usually kept on a shelf or a bedside table. Gods Word is an amenity for whatever ails us. Like a heaping helping of meat and vegetables, it warms us and fills us with exactly what we need. It fills me with joy.

God speaks to us through David or John or

Paul. Friends we come to know when we read the Bible. It provides us with a road map to lead us down the straight and narrow. The Word is *God Breathed (*2 Timothy 3:16) and can increase our faith.

The Bible has everything we look for in a good book. It has family love, war, romance, mystery, history, poetry, music and humor.

So, if your body is sick get a big bowl of comforting soup. For everything else take in a big helping of Gods comforting word!

Romans 15:4 For whatsoever things were written aforetime were written for our learning, that we through patience and comfort of the scriptures might have hope.

Chapter Seven

PRAISE

Sometimes Life is Just Hard

Father, my heart is heavy. Sometimes life is just hard. When I said good-bye to my sweet friend in the hospital yesterday, I had no way of knowing it would be our final good-bye. If I had known I would have lingered a little longer. Held his hand a little tighter. Said that prayer a little louder.

We talked about You, Father. But if I had known he would be leaving during the night we would have talked about You more. I would have sung that song to him he wanted to hear. Yes, even without the music.

He rode alone in the back of that ambulance to that big hospital in North Carolina; a hundred miles into the unknown. He didn't have to. I could have kept him company and sang his favorite hymns all the way there. I'm pretty sure it was not meant for me to go. I asked if he wanted me to and he said no. Probably Your way of sparing me the heartbreak of watching him pass. We just knew they would put a new heart into him. That he would come home like new and I would have to cook him chicken soup. That was the plan and I felt like I let him down. But it was not Your plan or I would have been there.

I will praise You still through the things that weigh me down and know in Your time You will lift the burden and add another layer to my joy.

Psalm 91:14-15 Because he hath set his love upon me, therefore will I deliver him: I will set him on high, because he hath known my name. He shall call upon me, and I will answer him: I will be with him in trouble; I will deliver him, and honour him.

Thank You for Answered Prayer

I am an enthusiastic list maker. There is just something about the satisfaction of checking things off a list in completion. It is a pleasurable sense of accomplishment as I go about my daily routine. I have an exhaustive list of chores. I list errands and I even have a list of those requesting prayer.

I have learned from my list of things to pray about to say thank You, Lord, for that healing touch, rather than telling Him that someone needs to be healed. He already knows that. We don't need to tell God how to do His work. God is in the details...every little one. Prayer is a form of worship. Remember to talk to Him often as He loves to hear from those who love Him and worship Him.

Philippians 4:6 Be careful for nothing; but in every thing by prayer and supplication with *thanksgiving* let your requests be made known unto God.

Never Too Young

A few years ago I had the most important job in the world. I was caregiver for two two-year-olds and two three-year-olds ten hours a day. Plus a precious five-year-old part time. Needless to say Monday through Friday was a whirlwind for me. Harmony requires much patience and a scheduled routine in this sort of setting.

Summer meant teaching them to swim. Then they took turns choosing the same Barney video every day. Besides storytime, playtime, naptime and potty training I wondered if these little ones were too young to teach the importance of daily prayer. As soon as this question entered my mind the answer followed. I remembered a poem prayer I had learned as a small child. I had not thought of it in years. So, before breakfast, lunch and snack time there was eight tiny hands clasped and four sweet souls (sometimes five) repeating after Nana the words of that prayer.

It must have been a joyful event for them because after the prayer was said they ignored the Amen and yelled, "YAY!" I started to correct them with the proper ending of *Amen*, but then I thought, *Why not get excited and happy about being thankful to God for His many blessings?*

Maybe instead of saying Amen at the end of our prayers, we should start saying, *YAY*!

Matthew 19:14 But Jesus said, Suffer little children, and forbid them not, to come unto me: for of such is the kingdom of heaven.

Adapting to Changes

There's a shift in the winds this morning. The taste of a new season in the air. Fall is not far away.

I am what people call *Old School*. Set in my ways and have never been fond of change. I enjoy a simplistic life and can't see any reason to change it. When things I enjoy begin to change the rebellious side of me rears it's ugly head. I don't want to lose the warm days full of sunshine!

It has been said that "*One of the reasons people resist change is because they focus on what they have to give up instead of what they have to gain.*" The fleshly, human side of me digs in my heels to keep things as they are. I eventually come around. I adjust to the difference and accept the change begrudgingly. Then I remember that our God is a God of change. *He* never changes, but He changes us.

The Bible tells us, *"To every thing there is a season, and a time to every purpose under the heaven."* It says *"The inward man is renewed day by day."* Paul tells us in 1 Corinthians *"We shall all be changed."* The one time I can say I truly embraced change was when the Holy Spirit stirred my heart causing me to come to Christ and I *was* changed.

I am glad the Lord brought this blunder to my attention. It is something I need to work on.

Lord, help me to see that change is necessary and to praise You through every one. I know it is possible I may be changed in the twinkling of an eye before I die. That is another change I will happily embrace.

2 Corinthians 5:17 Therefore if any man be in Christ, he is a new creature: old things are passed away; behold, all things are become new.

What Stress?

I read a quote by Corrie Ten Boom today, *"There is no panic in Heaven! God has no problems, only plans."* It caught my attention!

Seems like the words anxiety, stress and Zanax are much too common in today's world. We are running at a speed of life God did not intend for us to run. We rush out the door for work or school. We get frustrated and impatient in traffic that is moving too slow for our schedule. We yell at the kids for not being ready on time and insist they have their Pop Tart in the car. If we get a minute to relax and clear our thoughts, we squirm in the seat and wonder why we are waiting so long for the doctor to see us.

There is no *easy* fix for the sprint we run. But there is a way to remove much of the stress. We need to slow down! Maybe if we *plan* ahead of time. Do things to make the next day go smoother on the night before. Get up fifteen minutes earlier to spend time in prayer. Putting God first will certainly make the day go smoother. Praising Him through it all will remove the stress!

In the midst of making my lists and doing all that is on them. In the flurry of life's busyness. In that moment of hurry, hurry, hurry...remind me Lord of why I was put here in the first place. To worship and glorify You. Teach me how to slow down. To spend more of my time with You and to share You with others. Thank You, Lord, for the privilege.

Romans 12:2 And be not conformed to this world: but be ye transformed by the renewing of your mind, that ye may prove what is that good, and acceptable, and perfect, will of God.

Come to My Table

I enjoy cooking. Always have. Experiments in the kitchen have been interesting to say the least. Sometimes a happy success; sometimes not. Usually this undertaking is to create or improve on something for Sunday dinner. Occasional Sundays are a special time for gathering the family at Nana's house and everyone looks forward to it.

The children run and play, the ladies gather in the kitchen and the men retreat to the garage to discuss the latest project. When the meal is ready to be served I say, "Somebody tell the boys to come to the table." They are always happy to hear it.

When everyone is settled and Grace has been said, we enjoy each others company eating and laughing and talking.

I look forward to the day when I will be the one called to the table. I am a part of the Bride of Christ. Not a flower girl. Not a bridesmaid. But the Bride. United with all of His children at the consummation of the greatest marriage ceremony ever witnessed. Usually, the final element of a marriage ceremony concludes in a great feast. In Biblical times these feasts lasted for several days. There will be a wedding feast at the marriage supper of the Lamb and I will be there praising Him, not for several days, but for eternity!

Revelation 19:7-8 Let us be glad and rejoice, and give honour to him: for the marriage of the Lamb is come, and his wife hath made herself ready.

And to her was granted that she should be arrayed in fine linen, clean and white: for the fine linen is the righteousness of saints.

Learning to Talk

I've been told I learned to speak at an early age. I have loved words for as long as I can remember. I like to dissect them, spell them, utter them and learn new ones. At the age of sixteen I knew I was born to write. Even now I am teaching myself a new way of talking!

Words are used to express many things. They are our main way of communicating. Conversations, disagreements, sweet nothings, gossip. Guilty of gossip, I have had to repent and found it harder to forgive myself than to forgive others. The relationship to the one I spoke of has suffered and may never be the same. But even in a seasoned age I am still learning. Learning that when gossipy words cross my mind, I must turn my thoughts to words good and pure. I now try to speak favorable of everyone, or not at all.

I am learning to talk differently in my

prayer life as well. I have stopped trying to tell God what to do. Stopped telling Him what I need. Instead I say, "Thank You, Lord, for how You will handle this situation and I want only what You want. Thy will be done in every aspect of my life."

I don't always get it right. Sometimes I go back to the old way of talking. Old habits are hard to break. But God knows my heart and I will correct myself when it becomes necessary. Still learning to talk and praising Him through it all.

Proverbs 16:24 Pleasant words are as an honeycomb, sweet to the soul, and health to the bones.

DEBORAH NORTON

ABOUT THE AUTHOR

Deborah Norton currently resides in a small town in the upstate of South Carolina. A happy and loving mother of three and 'Nana' to many, she is passionate about life and advocates intervention whenever children are neglected or abused.

Made in the USA
Columbia, SC
11 September 2022